MINECRAFT HACKS

COMBAT EDITION

MINECRAFT HACKS

HACKS

COMBAT EDITION

THE UNOFFICIAL GUIDE TO TIPS AND TRICKS THAT OTHER GUIDES WON'T TEACH YOU

MEGAN MILLER

Sky Pony Press
New York

Copyright © 2014 by Hollan Publishing, Inc.

Sky Pony Press books may be purchased in bulk at special discounts for sales promotion, corporate gifts, fund-raising, or educational purposes. Special editions can also be created to specifications. For details, contact the Special Sales Department, Sky Pony Press, 307 West 36th Street, 11th Floor, New York, NY 10018 or info@skyhorsepublishing.com.

Sky Pony® is a registered trademark of Skyhorse Publishing, Inc.®, a Delaware corporation.

Minecraft® is a registered trademark of Notch Development AB.
The Minecraft game is copyright © Mojang AB.

Visit our website at www.skyponypress.com.

10 9 8 7 6 5 4 3 2 1

Manufactured in the United States of America, October 2014
This product conforms to CPSIA 2008

Library of Congress Cataloging-in-Publication Data is available on file.

Cover photo credit Megan Miller
Book design by Sara Kitchen

Print ISBN: 978-1-63450-101-9
Ebook ISBN: 978-1-63450-102-6

TABLE OF CONTENTS

INTRODUCTION

If you are new to the game, fighting the mobs in Minecraft can be a bit scary. But once you get used to the mobs and fighting them (and get used to occasionally dying!), it can be a lot of fun. I was not much of a fighter at first, but now I stay up at night (Minecraft night) just to find and kill some skellies, zombies, and Creepers. It's also a great way to get more experience points so you can enchant more weapons, armor, and tools.

This book has all the information you need to improve your fighting skills against the different mobs in Minecraft, from Blazes to zombie pigmen, and some tips to help you in PvP, as well. You'll learn more about your weapons, and how to enchant them and use potions. The mob profile pages examine each neutral and hostile mob: where you'll find it, how to kill it, and what experience points and drops it will give you. On each page you'll also find the number of strikes needed to kill a mob, and these are generally the minimum number of strikes needed. However, you may need fewer strikes if you use the critical hit tactic and more if the opponent wears armor, heals quickly, or if you don't have a fully charged bow.

As with pretty much everything, practice makes perfect. So to become a truly great fighter, get your sword and bow out and start taking out those mobs.

Note: The tips in this book are for the Minecraft PC game 1.8. If you are using a different version of Minecraft, some effects and behaviors may be slightly different. You can research any topic further by visiting the official Minecraft community wiki at Minecraft.gamepedia.com.

CHAPTER 1

SWORDS

Your primary Minecraft combat weapons are, of course, your sword and your bow. Your sword is for close combat, or melee, and your bow is for distance attacks. However, if you are caught unprepared—while harvesting a crop of melons, for example—you can use a tool if you have one; a pickaxe, axe, or shovel will deal more damage than your bare hands. There are other items in Minecraft you can use and build to inflict damage. Flint and steel and a bucket of lava are two popular warfare weapons.

The wooden sword is your first weapon, unless you are lucky and can get to stone quickly with your wooden pickaxe! One of your first goals in Survival mode should be to upgrade to a stone sword. Then continue upgrading until you have a couple of trusty enchanted diamond swords at your side. Left-click with a sword in hand to strike and right-click to block incoming strikes.

Crafting a Sword

You'll need two blocks of a single type of weapons material (wood planks, stone, gold ingot, iron ingot, or diamond ore) and one stick to make a sword. If you are making a wooden sword, you need to use the same kind of wood for both wood planks and the stick.

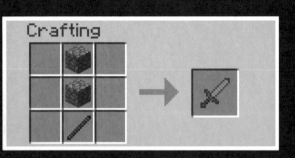

Sword recipe: 2 sword material + 1 stick.

You can also acquire weapons from killed mobs and from trading with villagers. Sometimes a zombie will spawn with a sword in hand or a skeleton may spawn with an enchanted bow. There's a chance they will drop the weapons when they die, and then they're yours.

Sword Damage

The amount of damage a sword can do depends on the material it is made of. Wooden swords deal the least damage, diamond the most. Compare the stats on the next page to using your bare hands, which causes 1 point of damage. Keep in mind that a heart is equal to 2 health points. Also notice that the golden sword gives the same damage as the wooden sword! It often makes sense to go from an iron sword straight to a diamond one, skipping the gold. You can increase the amount of damage you deal by using a critical hit, which you perform by jumping and then striking as you fall. A critical hit increases the damage by up to about 50 percent.

Material	Damage Points/ Hearts
Wooden Sword	5 points ❤❤❤
Stone Sword	6 points ❤❤❤
Iron Sword	7 points or ❤❤❤❤
Golden Sword	5 points ❤❤❤
Diamond Sword	8 points ❤❤❤❤

Sword Durability

Each weapon—and tool—has a limit on its use called its durability. Durability is measured in number of uses. By far the most durable swords are the diamond swords, which can last for more than 1,500 uses. Only your hands can last longer! Meanwhile, gold is not very durable at all and only lasts 33 uses. Once you've used a weapon the maximum number of times, it breaks and disappears. Here are the stats:

Sword Material	Uses
Wooden Sword	60
Stone Sword	132
Iron Sword	251
Golden Sword	33
Diamond Sword	1563

About Durability

Durability is how long a weapon or tool will last—how many chops, stabs, and swings at an item, mob, or player before it breaks. For example, an iron axe has a durability of 251, which means you can use it 251 times. When a weapon or tool breaks, it makes a clanking sound and disappears from your inventory. If you use a tool or weapon on an item it isn't meant for, like using a sword to break a dirt block, it usually counts as two uses rather than one. So it's good to use the right tool for the job, unless you are in a pickle.

You can quickly see how much you've used a weapon by looking at it in your inventory. At the bottom of the weapon's icon is the durability bar. The durability bar only shows up after you've used the weapon or tool for the first time, and it starts as a full green bar. As you use the weapon, the bar shortens and eventually turns red. Finally, the colored bar disappears, leaving an empty gray space when you are at the end of the weapon's lifetime. (However, you still have a couple of uses when the colored bar disappears. The number of uses remaining depends on the material. A gold weapon will have only 2 more uses while a diamond will have 61.

Under the sword, pickaxe, and bow you can see the durability bar.

You can also find out the exact durability remaining on any weapon in your inventory by turning durability tool tips on. To do this, press the F3 and H buttons at the same time. On a Mac, you may need to press the Fn, F3, and H buttons at the same time.

You can see exact durability in item tool tips if you press F3+H to turn this on.

CHAPTER 2

BOW AND ARROW

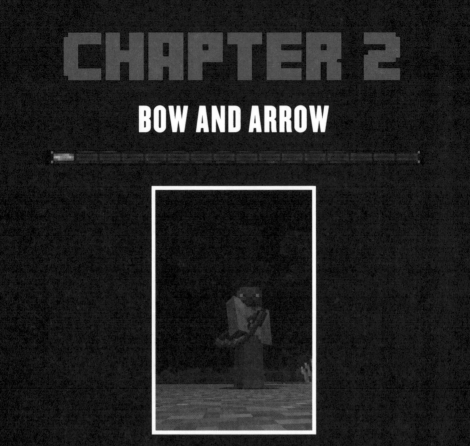

A bow and arrow is essential for killing mobs from a distance. If you have a chance to kill a mob from a little ways away, take it. This keeps you safe. However, you will still need to get up close to any dropped experience orbs to get the XP points.

Crafting a Bow and an Arrow

The hard part of bows and arrows is getting the resources to make enough of them, especially when you are at the start of your game. You will need three pieces of string, which you get fairly easily from killing spiders with your sword. In the daytime, big spiders are passive, and you can often find a couple spiders in the morning that spawned overnight around your house. They'll turn hostile when you strike your first blow, but at least you start out with the advantage.

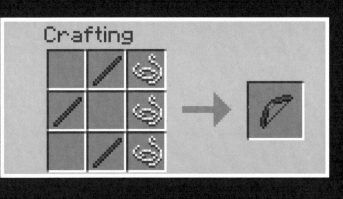

Craft a bow with 3 sticks + 3 string.

For arrows, you *can* gather some already made arrows by killing skeletons. Skeletons will randomly drop 0–2 arrows. However, unless you have a skeleton mob farm, you won't get enough arrows from killing skeletons alone. To make your own arrows, you need sticks, flint, and feathers. A flint, 1 stick, and 1 feather make 4 arrows. Ideally, you'll want to have between a half stack and a stack of arrows (32–64) on you pretty much all the time, depending on how often you use your bow. For 64 arrows, you'll need 16 pieces of flint and 16 feathers. And *that* means you'll need to shovel about 160 blocks of gravel and kill about 16 chickens. (You probably will want the Infinity enchantment for your bow as soon as possible! The Infinity enchantment gives you infinite arrows, as long as you keep one single arrow in your inventory.)

Craft arrows from 1 flint + 1 stick + 1 feather.

You can recover some arrows you have shot that missed their marks and landed in the ground or trees, but these won't be enough to keep you supplied. You can't recover any arrows shot by a skeleton or arrows shot while using the Infinity enchantment.

Bow Durability and Damage

An unenchanted bow will last for 385 uses.

Depending on the strength of your shot (how far you pull the bow back), a bow will cause 1–10 points of damage. You can achieve a critical hit with a bow by pulling it back all the way; this is also called a fully charged bow. The bow will shake a little when fully charged, and the arrow you release will leave a trail of tiny stars. A fully charged arrow can fly as far as 65 blocks. It will give 9 points of damage or, very occasionally, 10.

A fully charged arrow leaves a trail of stars.

About Damage

Each mob and player in Minecraft has a specified number of health points. Players have 20 health points, and these are represented in your heads-up display (HUD) as hearts. (Your HUD is the set of bars, stats, and inventory hotbar at the bottom of your screen.) A tiny slime block only has 1 point (half a heart) while the Wither boss has 300 points (150 hearts). Once a mob or player has no health points left, they die. When you strike a mob or player, the tool or weapon you use deals a specific amount of damage points. Each damage point takes away 1 health point. In addition to weapons and tools, things that can cause damage to a mob or player include fire, lava, lightning, cactus, TNT explosions, drowning, falling, suffocating, poison, starvation, the Thorns enchantment on another player's armor, the Wither effect, and just being in the Void. The Void is the empty space beyond bedrock. The land of The End is also surrounded by the Void.

Your HUD shows your health status, hunger status, and experience level above your inventory hotbar.

Repairing Weapons

You can repair weapons (or armor) by combining a used item with an identical new or used item on your crafting grid. It doesn't matter in which square of the crafting grid you place the two weapons. However, both weapons must be of the same material. Therefore, you can't combine a stone sword with a diamond one. The resulting weapon has the usage points of both weapons added together. If this totaled durability is less than the maximum durability a new version of the weapon would have, you also get a bonus of up to 5 percent of the total possible durability. To get the most benefit from that 5 percent bonus, repair two worn weapons whose added durability is 95 percent or less than full durability for the weapon. If you don't want to check points and do calculations, all you really have to do is make sure to repair one already worn weapon with another already worn weapon. Both weapons should show some of the green durability bar missing. Be careful not to repair an enchanted weapon on the grid. Doing this will remove the enchantments. To repair an enchanted weapon (or tool), you should use an anvil. See the chapter on enchanted weapons for more information.

Repair two used weapons to get bonus durability.

CHAPTER 3

OTHER WEAPONS

You aren't limited to the standard bow and sword for defeating your foes. You can use an interesting variety of other Minecraft items to damage or kill your enemies. Some are excellent substitutes for your sword or bow.

Tools

Axes, pickaxes, and shovels can deal more damage than your bare fists. Like swords, the weakest and least durable tools are made of wood, and the strongest and most damaging are made of diamond. However, they aren't as durable in combat as they are at their assigned task. If you use a tool rather than a weapon to strike a mob, it will count as two uses in durability, rather than one. Here's a breakdown of what they can do:

	Wood	Stone	Iron	Gold	Diamond
Axe Damage	4.5	5.5	6.5	4.5	7.5
Pickaxe Damage	4	5	6	4	7
Shovel Damage	3.5	4.5	5.5	3.5	6.5
Durability (Pickaxe, Axe, Shovel)	60	132	251	33	1562

Using a hoe is the same as using your hands. It doesn't do any more damage and doesn't register any durability hits if it isn't used to till dirt.

Bucket of Lava

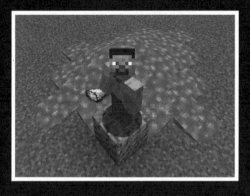

A bucket of lava is essential for your inventory. You do have to be careful about placing the lava, so you aren't damaged as well. It's best to hop up on a quickly placed block of gravel first. Buckets of lava are best poured at the last minute, so that the enemy is close by or doesn't have enough time to react. In the Overworld, lava will flow 3 blocks away from the block you pour it on. It will also burn most items in its path as well as any mob, except in the Nether. Nether mobs are not damaged by either lava or fire. Lava flows faster in the Nether than in the Overworld.

Flint and Steel

Flint and steel is a small tool crafted from an iron ingot and flint (you get flint from shoveling gravel). You place it on a block and right-click it to set it alight. You can use it against mobs by simply clicking the ground under their feet or the blocks in front of them if they are running. You can make a Creeper explode almost immediately by clicking it with flint and steel. Flint and steel has a durability of 65.

Anvil

Anvils are used primarily for repairing and enchanting weapons and armor. However, they have an interesting characteristic that makes them suitable as weapons. They respond to gravity, and if they are dropped from a good height, they will land with a force powerful enough to kill a mob or player. Anvils will cause approximately 2 points of damage per block fallen, up to a maximum of 40 points (20 hearts).

Anvil Traps: For a very simple anvil trap, you can place an anvil on top of a pillar of signs. This will get the anvil up high enough so that it will cause damage when it falls. At the bottom of the pillar, you need to create a way that a mob or player will break the block that the pillar stands on. When they do this, all the signs will drop, and so will the anvil. You must press Shift when you click to place signs (and the anvil) on top of each other like this. You also need to disguise the pillar of signs if you are trying this on other players in a PvP server. For example, the pillar could be just above a block of diamond in a fake mining corridor that you know players will travel down. Any player mining the diamond block from beneath will be hit. As an even simpler alternative, wait on top of a cliff or roof. Place the anvil in the same way you place gravel when you want it to fall—against another block. The anvil will drop heavily to the ground, injuring any player or mob in its way.

Cutaway of a simple anvil trap.

TNT

TNT is an explosive block in Minecraft. It will kill mobs or players close to it. You can find TNT at the bottom of desert temples or craft it from gunpowder (a drop from Creepers) and sand. To set it alight, you use flint and steel. This gives you a few seconds to run before it explodes. TNT can also be ignited with a flaming arrow, lava and fire, traveling over an activator rail in a minecart, a redstone pulse, dispensers, and more. TNT will destroy up to three-quarters of the blocks around it, unless it's in water. In water it won't destroy anything, but it will give an explosive sound. Two popular combat uses for TNT are TNT traps and TNT cannons.

TNT Trap: To make a TNT trap, place the TNT where you want it. Connect TNT to a trigger mechanism, like a pressure plate or a lever. A player or mob stepping on the pressure plate will start the TNT countdown. Or use a lever to ignite the TNT yourself.

Connect a pressure plate to TNT with redstone. You will want to hide the redstone trail, though!

Arrow Dispenser Trap

An automatic arrow dispenser is another common weapon used in a variety of creative ways in Minecraft. For a simple one that dispenses one arrow at a time, use redstone to connect a dispenser to a pressure plate. The pressure plate should be a short distance away from but right in front of the dispenser's mouth. There is an example on the following page. Once you have it working, you can cover up the redstone with other blocks to hide it. This is something you could place in a corridor in your home to deter intruders!

Simple arrow dispenser.

CHAPTER 4

ARMOR

Armor is essential in combat. While you can survive occasional attacks from lesser mobs without it, it is armor that lets you survive big damage attacks and continue fighting. Armor protects you from sword or contact attacks from mobs and other players, as well as from arrows, fire, lava, fishing rods, Ghast or Blaze fire balls, fire charges, cactus damage, and explosions. It doesn't protect you from drowning, suffocating, falling, status effects, extended fire exposure, the Void, or Potions of Harming.

Crafting armor requires 24 pieces of the same material, either leather, gold, iron, or diamond. You can't craft chainmail armor, but you can trade villagers for it. Rarely, a skeleton or zombie wearing chainmail armor will drop it when killed.

Full suit of chainmail armor.

Each piece of armor provides 1–8 defense points. Each defense point gives a reduction of 4 percent on incoming damage. On your HUD, you can see the total number of defense points your current armor will provide. A chestplate icon is equal to 2 defense points. The separate armor pieces don't protect specific parts of your body, they just add up total defense points. So if you are just starting out and are very poor on materials, you can start with leather boots or a leather helmet. The boots cost 4 leather, whereas it costs 5 leather for the helmet. They both give 1 point of defense, but the boots will last longer. From the charts below, you can work out which pieces of armor you can afford and what will give you the most protection and last the longest.

Protection from Full Sets of Armor

Material	Full Set Protection	Damage Reduction
Leather		28%
Golden		44%
Chain		48%
Iron		60%
Diamond		80%

Individual Armor Defense Points

	Leather	Gold	Chainmail	Iron	Diamond
Helmet	1	2	2	2	3
Chestplate	3	5	5	6	8
Leggings	2	3	4	5	6
Boots	1	1	1	2	3

Durability

Armor durability is lowered by weapon or melee attacks, explosions, lava, and fire. The greatest damage done to your armor is by TNT explosions or Creeper explosions, but you can halve the durability hit by blocking with your sword. Each attack counts as 1 hit, and 1 point will be taken from the durability of each separate piece of armor. Once the durability of armor reaches 0, the bar disappears and you can use it one more time. Also, if you are using armor that reduces damage, the armor will reduce in durability when you take (and it repels) damage.

	Leather	Gold	Chainmail or Iron	Diamond
Helmet	56	78	166	364
Chestplate	81	113	241	529
Leggings	76	106	226	496
Boots	66	92	196	430

With Minecraft 1.8, you can place your armor on armor stands.

Horse Armor

In chests found in dungeons, temples, and mineshafts, as well as village blacksmith shops, you can find horse armor. There are three types of horse armor. Iron armor gives the horse 20 percent protection, gold gives 28 percent, and diamond 44 percent. Although you can't enchant it, horse armor has unlimited durability, so you don't have to repair it.

Horse with diamond armor.

CHAPTER 5

ENCHANTING

Enchanting and brewing potions aren't easy to do at the beginning of the game. Usually these activities will have to wait until you've gathered the proper resources. However, getting to this level should be a major goal if you want to survive well in Normal or Hard mode. Enchanted weapons and armor make a huge difference in surviving combat, as can potions. They are absolutely necessary for fighting the strongest mobs, like the Ender Dragon and Wither.

Enchanting comes before brewing potions, because you don't have to go to the Nether to start enchanting. To start enchanting, you need an enchantment table, which you craft from obsidian, books, and diamonds, and lapis lazuli to pay for the enchantments. The levels of enchantment you can give to an item are increased by surrounding the table with up to 15 book-shelves. There are different levels for enchantments. For example, a Protection IV enchantment will give more protection than a Protection I enchantment.

Crafting an enchantment table.

To enchant, click on the enchanting table and place the item you want to enchant in the left slot. In the right panel, you'll be given three choices of enchantment. It will tell you how many experience levels you need to perform the enchantment, as well as how much lapis lazuli (and how many experience levels) it will cost. Select the enchantment you want on the right and then remove your enchanted item. Sometimes you will get additional enchantments with the one you picked. Enchanted items have a magical glow.

In the enchanting screen, you can mouse over the three enchanting options for a tooltip that shows what one of the enchantments will be.

The higher your experience level (shown in your green experience bar), the more XP points you need to get to the next level. Because the best enchantments require level 30, you should stop and enchant something whenever you get to level 30. Going from level 27 back to level 30 is faster than going from level 30 to 33.

Armor Enchantments

The **Protection** enchantment reduces any kind of damage. **Fire Protection** reduces damage from fire, and **Blast Protection** reduces damage from explosions. **Projectile Protection** protects you from damage from arrows and Ghast or Blaze fireballs. **Feather Falling** (boots only) reduces damage from falls. **Depth Strider** (boots only) allows you to move more quickly in water. **Respiration** (helmet only) helps you breathe and see under water. **Aqua Affinity** (helmet only) makes it easier to mine underwater. **Thorns** inflicts a small amount of damage on anyone attacking you. Of all these, Protection is often the best, because it gives you general protection from almost everything. However, once you start getting lots of diamonds, you can think about creating different suits for armor for different occasions: visiting the Nether, fighting guardians, or caving.

Enchanted armor can help you move, breathe, and mine underwater.

Sharpness increases damage. **Smite** increases damage more, but only to undead mobs, and **Bane of Arthropods** does the same for spiders, silverfish, and Endermites. **Fire Aspect** will light your target on fire, and **Knockback** will knock him, her, or it back. **Looting** gives a chance of getting better drops from your hostile mobs. Of all these, choose Sharpness over Smite and Bane of Arthropods. Looting is also very helpful for getting those rare drops.

Bow Enchantments

Power increases damage, while **Punch** gives more knockback. **Flame** will send a flaming arrow to deal fire damage. **Infinity** means you need only a single arrow in your inventory to shoot as much as you want. Of all these, choose Infinity if you have any issues with arrow making, and then Power.

Using Gold

It might seem from all the stats that gold is a waste of time as a weapons or tool material. It has terrible durability, and a golden sword doesn't do more damage than the lowly wooden sword. However, gold has a special attribute that you should keep in mind. It is more "enchantable"—you can get better enchantments for the same XP cost as another material. That means you are more likely to get Sharpness IV at your enchanting table with a golden sword than a diamond sword.

Repairing Enchanted Weapons

Anvils allow you to repair an enchanted weapon and keep its enchantments. You do this by placing your worn item on the left and either a new item of the same material on the right or, in some cases, the material the item is made of, like diamond or iron. You can also combine two enchanted weapons of the same material to combine enchantments. An anvil also allows you to combine an unenchanted weapon with an enchanted book to place the book's enchantment on the weapon. If you combine two similar items with the same enchantment level, the resulting item will be given the next level enchantment, if there is a next level. For example, you can combine two Sharpness IV swords to make a Sharpness V sword.

Repairing with the anvil will also cost experience levels; here it is just one level

CHAPTER 6

POTIONS

Potions will help you in battle tremendously. They can restore your health, make you invisible, or make you faster and stronger. They are a must when you are fighting boss mobs like the Wither. You will be ready to start making potions when you start visiting the Nether and killing the mobs there, as they supply much of what you need. For example, to make a brewing stand, you'll need a Blaze rod dropped by a Blaze. When you have drunk a potion, a notice shows up on your inventory screen along with how long the potion will last, if it isn't an instant potion.

Brewing

First you brew bottles of water and another ingredient to create a "base" potion. This ingredient is almost always Nether wart, and this brew is called the Awkward Potion. Then you brew your base potion with a new ingredient to make a primary potion, which will give the drinker a special status effect, like Speed, for a certain amount of time.

Brewing the Awkward Potion with Nether wart and water.

Then, if you want, you can brew your primary potion again with a modifying ingredient to create a secondary potion. Use glowstone to make the effect stronger, gunpowder to make it into a splash potion, or redstone to make the potion's effect last longer. Glowstone and redstone cancel each other's effect. In many cases, you can add fermented spider eye to a potion to reverse its effects and make it into a harming potion.

Brewing the Potion of Regeneration with a Ghast tear and the Awkward Potion base.

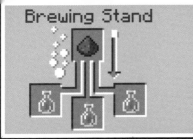

Brewing Stand

Modifying the Potion of Regeneration by brewing it with gunpowder to make a splash potion.

Weaponized Potions

With a splash potion, you can use the potion as a weapon. The splash potion looks a little like a grenade, with a pin at the top. Splash potions are much more effective when they are thrown at the hitbox of the mob or player, rather than an adjacent block, like the block the mob is standing on. Think of the hitbox as an invisible box around an entity or item that defines where it can be struck or clicked on. Be careful of using potions on the undead, though. On skeletons, zombies, and the like, splash potions can work in reverse. A Potion of Harming will heal a skeleton, a Potion of Healing will harm it, and a Potion of Regeneration won't have any effect. The undead, spiders, and the Ender Dragon also won't be affected by poisonous potions.

Basic Potions and Ingredients

Awkward (Base Potion)	Water and Nether Wart
Fire Resistance	Magma Cream
Healing	Glistering Melon

Leaping	Rabbit's Foot
Night Vision	Golden Carrot
Poison	Spider Eye
Regeneration	Ghast Tear
Strength	Blaze Powder
Swiftness	Sugar
Water Breathing	Pufferfish
Harming	Potion of Water Breathing or Poison + Fermented Spider Eye
Slowness	Potion of Swiftness or Fire Resistance + Fermented Spider Eye
Weakness	Doesn't Use Awkward Potion as a Base, Just Water with Fermented Spider Eye

CHAPTER 7

FIGHTING TECHNIQUES

You can improve your combat skills by practicing some basic techniques. Certain techniques work better for specific situations than others.

Blocking: You can prevent up to 50 percent of damage from an incoming strike by right-clicking to block the attack.

Right-click with your sword to block damage from incoming attacks.

Block-Hitting: To block-hit with your sword, click right and left at same time, or alternate between these two. This can help you keep striking quickly while still protecting against your opponent's strikes. However, when you block you are moving slower, so this tactic is best used when you don't anticipate having to run around. Also, if your opponent can't see you, they can't hit you, so there's no need to block-hit when you are behind someone, for example.

Knockback: To knock-back an opponent, sprint to them and hit them while sprinting. This can knock a player back almost twice as far as regular hit. The only mobs you don't want to use this against are skeletons (this can give them time to recharge their bows) and any mob that you have difficulty catching.

Encircling: Circle around your enemy. This makes it harder for them to hit you. If you can keep behind the other player or mob, you can deliver damage while they can't.

Critical Hits: When you are falling through the air, you deliver up to 50 percent more damage to foes. Jump, and as you fall, strike. You can practice these as you slaughter your herd of cows or pigs.

Jump, then strike as you fall for a critical hit, which will show stars around your foe.

Strafing: If your enemy is using a bow or other projectiles, use your A and D keys to move left and right as you approach your enemy to make it harder for them to hit you.

Sword Timing: Check your sword timing. If you click very fast, Minecraft's sword animation can't keep up with your speed. When you see this happening, the game is dropping some of your sword hit clicks to keep up. If it's not animating a click, your sword isn't damaging your opponent. If you click a little slower, you can see that for each click, an animation occurs, and each click will count. This can actually improve your clicking/ hitting rate.

Aiming: When you aim with your bow (or with any projectile), take into account the direction your opponent is moving. If they are moving to your right, aim a little right, so they walk into your arrow. If you are waiting for an opponent to come into view, prepare by charging your bow, and keeping it extended, until they appear and you can shoot a critical arrow hit, practically before they even notice you. If you are fighting up close and using your arrow, you may not have time to fully charge your bow. Charge it halfway by pulling for a couple counts and then shooting and recharging.

Arrows fall as they fly, so aim above your target. Practice will help make you perfect.

Stunning with Fishing Rods: Many Minecraft PvP warriors like to use fishing rods in combat. Right-clicking your opponent as you run toward or away from them stuns them for a moment, allowing you more time to attack them or to escape.

Hide Surprise Weapons: If you are about to use flint and steel, or a bucket of lava, don't hold it until the last minute. When you hold it, your opponent will see it in your hands and know what you are about to do. This can give them a chance to escape. Use the number keys on top of your keyboard, 1–9, to switch quickly between weapons.

Ender Pearl Escape: You can use Ender Pearls to teleport anywhere you can aim the Pearl. It will damage you slightly, but much less than a fall from a height, a fall into lava, or a melee in which you are outgunned or outnumbered.

Water Fighting: If you can get your opponent into water, that will slow them down. If you are both in water, get below them. Your reach is longer from this angle than from the position above, so you can avoid their swings while still hitting them.

Keep Eating: Your hunger level is the most important thing in making sure you heal quickly. Make sure you have plenty of good food, like steaks or baked potatoes, to eat when your hunger drops.

Practice: Set up a world where your only goal is to fight, die, and fight again. If you turn cheats on, you can use Creative mode to gather armor, food, weapons, and more into chests. That way, when you switch to Hard mode, you won't have to spend time roasting that cow and can concentrate on fighting.

CHAPTER 8

THE MOBS YOU FIGHT

The word *mob* is short for mobile. Mobile was used in early multiple-player gaming to describe any entity that could move.

Mob Types

In Minecraft, mobs can be classed in several ways, like how aggressive they are or where they spawn.

Passive mobs, like chickens, will never attack you; other passive mobs include bat, chicken, cow, horse, mooshroom, ocelot, pig, rabbit, sheet, squid, and villager.

Neutral mobs are passive except in certain circumstances, when they become hostile. Neutral mobs are the cave spider (at high light levels), Enderman, spider (at high light levels), wolf, and zombie pigman.

Hostile mobs, like Creepers, attack you without being provoked. They include the Blaze, baby zombie, chicken jockey, Creeper, Elder Guardian, Endermite, Ghast, Guardian, Killer Bunny, magma cube, silverfish, skeleton, slime, spider jockey, witch, Wither, Wither skeleton, zombie, and zombie villager.

Darkness mobs spawn in low light levels in the Overworld. Darkness mobs include the Enderman, skeleton, Creeper, spider, and zombie.

The Darkness mobs come out at night.

Nether mobs spawn only in the Nether. Nether mobs include the Ghast, magma cube, and zombie pigman.

Local mobs spawn in specific areas in the Overworld or Nether. Overworld local mobs are cave spiders, slimes, silverfish, and witches. Nether local mobs are Wither skeletons and Blazes.

Utility mobs are mobs that were created to serve. Iron and snow golems are utility mobs. Iron golems can spawn naturally in large villages, and protect villagers by attacking hostile mobs. Snow golems can only be created by the player, and they also attack most mobs.

Iron and snow golems can help you out in a pinch.

Boss mobs have a more complicated programming than other types of mobs and are able to heal themselves. They have very high levels of health and attack strengths, so they are difficult to kill. Boss mobs include the Ender Dragon and the Wither.

Hostile Mob Behavior

Hostile mobs spawn within 24–128 blocks of a player. Most can see any player that is within 16 blocks of them; some can see further. When a mob sees the player in its line of sight (there are no opaque blocks in the way), it begins to pursue the player. If a hostile mob is 128 blocks away from a player, it will despawn or disappear. However, if you put a nametag on a mob, it won't despawn. Some hostile mobs can spawn with or pick up weapons and armor, and if they have these, they also won't despawn.

Once they spawn, they walk around randomly. However, if there is no player nearby (within 32 blocks), they'll stop walking after about 5 seconds and just stand still.

Almost all mobs are vulnerable to the same things players are: drowning, lava, suffocation, cactus, TNT explosions, and fall damage. Mobs are also damaged by fire, except for Nether mobs, who live in the fiery biome of Hell and are used to such things.

Almost all mobs are vulnerable to the same kinds of damage players are. These Creepers have been caught in lava.

CHAPTER 9

BABY ZOMBIES AND CHICKEN JOCKEYS

Baby Zombies

aby zombies are miniature zombies. There are baby ver-
sions of zombies, zombie villagers, and zombie pigmen,
and they all behave pretty much exactly the same way. About
5 percent of zombies spawn as baby zombies. The drops the
babies give are the same as for their adult version. They can be
equipped and pick up armor or weapons like the adults.

A baby zombie villager and a baby zombie pigman.

Chicken Jockeys

A chicken jockey is a baby zombie, baby zombie villager, or baby zombie pigman riding a chicken. They are very rare. There is a 5 percent chance that a baby zombie will spawn as a chicken jockey. This works out to a 0.25 percent chance for a chicken jockey to spawn. That's means about 1 in every 400 zombies will be a chicken jockey. However, if there are chickens nearby when the baby zombie spawns, its chance of becoming a chicken jockey are almost doubled.

A chicken jockey.

Baby zombies and chicken jockeys may be cute, but they're harder to fight than the slow adults. They are very fast!

If the baby's riding a chicken, you can't kill it by pushing it over a cliff. The chicken can just flutter slowly down to the ground without it or its rider being harmed. If a chicken jockey comes into contact with flowing water, it separates into the baby zombie and the chicken.

BABY ZOMBIE STATS

Mob Type: Hostile, Darkness

Health: Chicken – 4

Baby Zombie – 20

Attack Strength:

Easy – 2

Normal – 9

Hard – 13

Experience: Up to 22 (12 for baby zombie; 10 for a chicken)

Drops: Rotten flesh, 1 raw chicken, 0–2 feathers, more rarely 1 carrot, 1 potato, any armor or weapons it holds, 1 iron ingot, or 1 gold ingot (for a baby zombie pigman)

Spawn: Baby zombies and chicken jockeys spawn in the Overworld at light level 7 or below. Baby zombie pigmen spawn in the Nether.

Sword Strikes to Kill (Baby Zombie):

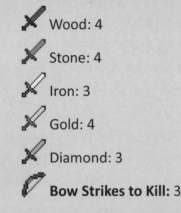

Wood: 4

Stone: 4

Iron: 3

Gold: 4

Diamond: 3

Bow Strikes to Kill: 3

Fighting a Baby Zombie or Chicken Jockey

To fight these kids, you will need to use your sword, because they run so fast. They are pretty hilarious, but if you don't pay attention they can still kill you. Although they spawn at low light levels, they don't burn in daylight, and they can also run through 1x1-block gaps. The best way to defeat a chicken jockey or baby zombie, once it has set its mark on you, is to attack as fast as you can. If you can, get two straight blocks above the baby zombie (by pillaring with two blocks of gravel, for example) and strike it from there.

CHAPTER 10

BLAZE

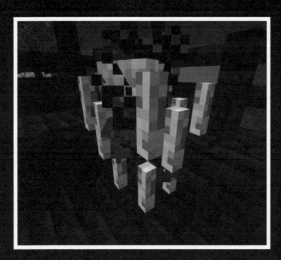

Blazes are hostile mobs found in Nether fortresses. They have a body made of dark gray smoke surrounded by three sections of four whirling golden rods. They are fierce opponents. Once they see you, they fly up in the air, catch on fire for a moment, and then rapidly hurl three fire charges at you. They'll repeat these actions over and over again. While it might seem best to avoid blazes entirely, they drop blaze rods, which are essential for several Minecraft activities. You need one blaze rod to make a brewing station for potion, and blaze powder makes the Potion of Fire Resistance. You also need blaze powder to make Eyes of Ender, which you are required to find and repair the End portal.

Blazes can spawn randomly in Nether fortresses, but you will also find special rooms in a fortress that house Blaze spawners. These rooms are up a short flight of stairs and have short walls topped by Nether fence.

A Blaze spawner in a Nether fortress.

BLAZE STATS

Mob type: Hostile, Nether, Local

Health: 20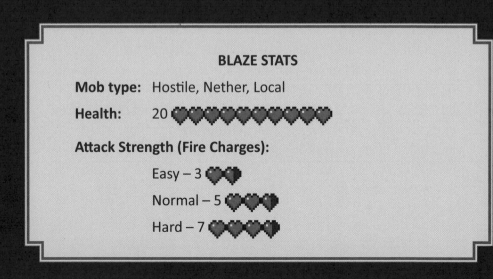

Attack Strength (Fire Charges):

Easy – 3

Normal – 5

Hard – 7

Attack Strength (From Contact):

Easy – 4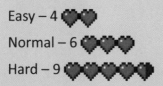

Normal – 6

Hard – 9

Experience: 10

Drops: 0–1 Blaze rods (in console edition may drop 0–2 glowstone dust)

Spawn: In Nether fortresses randomly or through a Blaze spawner, at low light levels (11 or less)

Sword Strikes to Kill:

Wood: 4, but don't bother if you don't have armor and strong swords. Unless you're on Easy, you'll be quickly overpowered and killed by fire damage, both from the fire charges and from contact by the Blazes.

Stone: 4

Iron: 4

Gold: 4

Diamond: 3

Fighting the Blaze

The Blaze is one of the more difficult mobs to fight. It flies up and down and back and forth, often out of reach. It fires its charges at you very quickly, and when it is on fire itself, it will give you significant fire damage when it touches you. A fire re-sistance potion will protect you greatly from the Blaze. Howev-er, to make potions, you first need a Blaze rod to create a brew-ing station. So if you have not killed any Blazes yet, you will not be able to make potions. In this case, you can use an enchanted golden apple, which gives you several status effects for a short time, including Absorption, Regeneration, Resistance, and five minutes of Fire Resistance.

After hurling its charges, the Blaze needs a few seconds to recharge.

Surprisingly, snowballs are a pretty good tactic to use against Blazes. Snowballs only do damage to two mobs, the Blaze and the Ender Dragon. They deliver 3 points of damage to the Blaze and 1 to the Dragon. A common tactic is to throw snowballs at the Blaze initially, and then run in with your sword to kill it. If you have Fire Resistance from a potion, you can also try hooking it with a fishing rod to bring it close and then attack with your sword. Blazes are also damaged by water, but water sizzles and disappears in the Nether.

Once a Blaze spawns, you have a few seconds while it gets ready to deliver the fire charges. After it hurls the charges (which it will only do if you are in its line of sight and within 16 blocks), it will take another few seconds to recharge. Use these moments to deliver as much damage as you can. If you can hide behind a block, you can pop out to draw the blaze's fire, hide again to dodge the charges, then come back out to attack during the short lull. However, this is much harder to do when you have multiple Blazes bearing down on you!

You can also create a space whereby you are below the Blaze, protected by blocks such as Nether brick, with just a one block gap that allows you to strike the Blaze with your sword. If another mob, like a Wither skeleton, is nearby, hide behind it. If you are lucky, the Blaze will hit the skeleton, which will then attack the Blaze. Once they are engaged, you can attack the Blaze yourself.

CHAPTER 11

CAVE SPIDER

Like their larger cousin, the spider, the cave spider is a neutral mob in light levels of 12 and above, and hostile at lower levels. It looks just like a regular spider, but it has a bluish fur and is smaller and faster. It is also poisonous on Normal and Hard difficulty levels. However, they don't spawn naturally like other mobs, they only spawn from spawners found in abandoned mineshafts. You can identify a cave spider spawner by the masses of cobwebs surrounding it. These mob spawners themselves look like a cage the size of a block with a miniature mob spinning around inside. Cave spiders, like spiders, can climb blocks vertically, like climbing a ladder.

Cave spiders are smaller than the regular spider, taking up less than a full 1x1 block of space. This means they can fit through a space as small as a block wide and a half block tall. Because of their small size and speed, they can be difficult to defeat.

CAVE SPIDER STATS

Mob Type: Neutral, Local

Health: 12 pts

Attack strength:

Easy – 2 ♥

Normal – 2 (with venom) ♥

Hard – 3 (with venom) ♥♥

Experience: 5 pts

Drops: 0–2 string, 0–1 spider eye

Spawn: Spawn in abandoned mineshafts only, at low light levels

Sword Strikes to Kill:

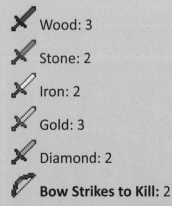

Wood: 3

Stone: 2

Iron: 2

Gold: 3

Diamond: 2

Bow Strikes to Kill: 2

Fighting the Cave Spider

To defeat the cave spider, you need to kill existing and spawning spiders and disable or destroy the spawner itself. Because they are so fast, you will be using a sword against them instead of the bow, which takes several moments to pull and charge before you can fire an arrow.

You will find yourself trying to battle these spiders at the same time as trying to destroy enough cobwebs around the spawner so that you can disable it. You can use a bucket of water to remove cobwebs, and shears are the fastest tool to cut them. Water will also uproot any torches placed on the ground, so be aware of where your torches are. One tactic is to close off the ends of the corridor they are in, and then tunnel in just above or below the spawner, so you can quickly destroy it with your pickaxe or place torches on each side. Placing torches will create enough light that it prevents spiders from spawning, disabling it.

Disarming a cave spider spawner.

Try to avoid letting these spiders get above you, where they can jump on you and damage you. The venom from their bite will cause you enough damage to bring you down to a half-heart of health. It won't kill you, but it will leave you very vulnerable to dying from anything else. Once you are bitten, retreat and use potions or milk to heal before you strike again. If you don't care about losing the spawner or any drops and experience points, you can pour a bucket of lava on it.

CHAPTER 12

CREEPER

reepers are one of the four main hostile mobs you encounter in the Overworld. The other three are skeletons, spiders, and zombies. Creepers are mottled green, have four tiny rectangular legs, and spawn in low light levels. Unlike zombies and skeletons, they don't die in the sunlight—although we all wish they would.

The biggest problem with Creepers is their silence. You can hear a zombie's groans and the scritching sound of a spider, but Creepers are very nearly silent. If you are lucky, you may hear a little rustle. But unless you are facing toward them as they approach, the last thing you will hear is the sizzle of a fuse burning before the Creeper explodes a block away from you, taking you down with it.

If the Creeper has been hit by lightning, it becomes the even deadlier charged Creeper. A charged Creeper has a bluish tinge flowing around it to signify the electric charge. Its explosion causes more damage than a TNT explosion.

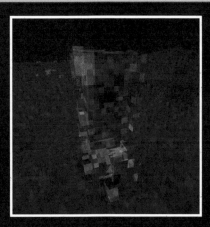

A charged Creeper.

Once either type of Creeper spots you (you have to be within 16 blocks), it will chase you. When it is within a block of you, it will start to sizzle and swell. And once it starts to sizzle, it will explode in 1.5 seconds. If you get away from it (about 3–5 blocks, depending on your difficulty level) within 1 second, the Creeper will not explode.

A swelling Creeper on the left and an exploding Creeper on the right.

CREEPER STATS

Mob Type: Hostile, Darkness

Health: 20

Attack Strength (Maximum):

Normal – 49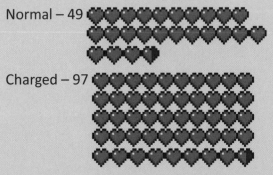

Charged – 97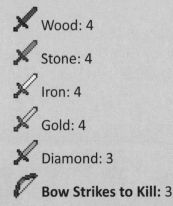

Drops: 0–2 gunpowder, a music disc (if killed by a skeleton), and a Creeper head (if killed by a charged Creeper).

Spawn: In the Overworld at light levels of 7 and below.

Sword Strikes to Kill:

Wood: 4

Stone: 4

Iron: 4

Gold: 4

Diamond: 3

Bow Strikes to Kill: 3

Fighting the Creeper

The best way to kill a Creeper is with your bow and arrow, keeping well away from it. If you can't do this, sprint straight to the Creeper and strike it with your sword. Striking it while you sprint will knock it back more than if you don't sprint. The moment you hit the Creeper, press S to move backward immediately. It is better to move backward after you've knocked the Creeper back, rather than try to angle left or right. If you move forward, you will still be too close to it. You can also do this maneuver without sprinting, but the timing is more critical. In either case, repeat the swoop in, smack back, and swoop out procedure until the Creeper dies. You may want to practice ahead of time switching quickly from the W key to move forward and the S key to move back.

As with most mob killing, the best sword enchantment for Creeper killing is Sharpness and the best bow enchantment is Power. If you can add knock back via the Knockback (sword) or Punch (bow) enchantment, that is also a big help, especially for the swoop in and out tactic.

CHAPTER 13

ELDER GUARDIAN

The Elder Guardian (a larger, more powerful version of the Guardian) is an ocean-dwelling hostile mob that appears with a new ocean monument structure. There are three Elder Guardians spawned with each ocean monument, and they will not respawn if you kill them. They live inside the monument. One is in a top room near the monument's treasure (8 gold blocks, hidden by prismarine blocks); the other two live in rooms on opposite wings of the monument.

You can find the rare ocean monument in deep ocean.

The Elder Guardian is very similar to the Guardian; it attacks in the same way, by laser and its defensive spines, but it deals more damage. It gives the same drops with one additional possibility, the wet sponge. Also like the Guardian, it swims suddenly and quickly and attacks both players and squid. Guardians will swim away from an approaching player to gain some range for its laser beam. However, the Elder Guardian has the unique ability to inflict players within a 50-block radius with Mining Fatigue III for five minutes. This is a status effect that will really slow down your mining, making it very difficult to break blocks. When the mob inflicts you with this, you'll see a shadowy image of the Elder Guardian on your screen for a moment.

ELDER GUARDIAN STATS

Mob Type: Hostile, Local

Health: 80 ♥♥♥♥♥♥♥♥♥♥
♥♥♥♥♥♥♥♥♥♥

Attack Strength:

Easy – 5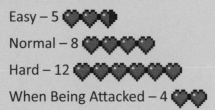

Normal – 8

Hard – 12

When Being Attacked – 4

Experience: 10

Drops: 0–1 raw fish, 0–2 prismarine shards, 0–1 prismarine crystals, 0–1 wet sponges; more rarely, it will drop raw salmon, clownfish, or pufferfish.

Spawn: Spawns only at an ocean monument, and only once with each ocean monument. Unlike other hostile mobs, they don't despawn, except in Peaceful level.

Sword Strikes to Kill:

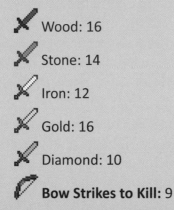

Wood: 16

Stone: 14

Iron: 12

Gold: 16

Diamond: 10

Bow Strikes to Kill: 9

As with fighting the Guardian, you will need to prepare your armor and potions for fighting and moving underwater: Aqua Affinity, Respiration, and Depth Strider enchantments, and Potions of Swiftness, Night Vision, and Water Breathing. You can also use Potion of Invisibility to prevent the Guardians from seeing and attacking you; this is a good tactic.

The Elder Guardian will inflict you with mining fatigue to prevent you from mining to find the hidden blocks of gold.

Like fighting the Guardian, your best move is to attack quickly and attack hard with your sharpest enchanted sword. Because of the Mining Fatigue, you likely won't be able to mine to find the gold blocks hidden in the middle of the monument, so your first goal is to take out the three Elder Guardians.

CHAPTER 14

ENDER DRAGON

The Ender Dragon is a large black dragon with reddish purple eyes. It is the largest mob in the game, over 20 blocks long. There is only one Ender Dragon, and it is found in the End, a world you travel to through the End portal.

The End is an island made of a special block called End stone, and tall columns of obsidian rise from the ground. The island floats in an endless dark space called the Void. If you fall off the edges of the island and into the Void, you will die. The Ender Dragon flies among the tops of several obsidian columns that have special blocks of crystals on top of them. These crystals regenerate the Dragon's health when it is injured, making it very difficult to slay the Dragon.

When the Ender Dragon is close to you, its purple health bar appears at the top of your screen. When it attacks you, the Ender Dragon flies right at you. It destroys all blocks besides obsidian and End stone in its path and causes damage to you when it hits you, as well as knocks you back. It may fly off for a little while, but will return to attack you again.

ENDER DRAGON STATS

Mob Type: Boss

Health: 200 ♥♥♥♥♥♥♥♥♥♥

Attack Strength:

      Easy – 6 ♥♥♥

      Normal – 10 ♥♥♥♥♥

      Hard – 15 ♥♥♥♥♥♥♥♥

Experience: 12,000

Drops: Dragon egg

Spawn: Only once, in the End

Sword Strikes to Kill:

Wood: 40 (These Strikes to Kill stats are purely theoretical. Because of the way the Ender Dragon heals itself and flies quickly, you will need an enchanted diamond sword and enchanted bow to kill the Dragon, and you may strike many more times than this in the game, because you will miss often.)

Stone: 34

 Iron: 29

Gold: 40

Diamond: 25

Bow Strikes to Kill: 23

Fighting the Ender Dragon

Before you go to the End, you must be prepared. First, you want to make the portal room safe and place chests to hold extra supplies. Then place a bed and sleep there to reset your spawn point. That way, if you die without killing the Dragon, you can enter the End again quickly with new supplies.

For supplies, you will need enchanted diamond armor, diamond swords, and enchanted bows. Plan on bringing an extra set of armor, three swords, and three bows. Because you will be fighting for a long time, you need several stacks of arrows or the Infinity enchantment on the bow. You will also want to bring at least a stack of obsidian to create a bridge from your spawn point to the main island and safe platforms. In addition to plenty of food, other supplies to consider are several stacks of snowballs, the makings for an army of iron and snow golems, and Potions of Healing and Regeneration.

To fight the Ender Dragon you must first destroy its healing crystals, which are on top of obsidian pillars. They look like cubes rotating in fire. You can also tell a crystal is present when a damaged Dragon flies by one and the crystal emits a ray to heal it. To destroy the crystal, you can throw any projectile at it, even projectiles that don't do damage. You can use your bow and arrow or throw snowballs or eggs. If you hit the crystal, it explodes with more force than TNT, so you don't want to be close! You may want to climb other obsidian pillars and make a safe ledge area using obsidian to fire on other crystals.

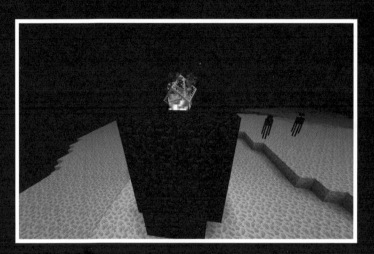

These crystals heal the Dragon, making it very difficult to kill. You'll have to destroy these first.

You will also have to deal with hordes of Endermen wandering around. You don't want to provoke them by looking at them, but it's easy to make a mistake. To prevent them from seeing you look at them, you can wear a pumpkin as a helmet. However, this also limits your ability to see well. To keep them occupied, you can unleash armies of iron and snow golems who will attack Endermen automatically and distract them. You could use a Potion of Invisibility, but this doesn't work on the Ender Dragon and you also need to remove your armor for it to work.

Once you've destroyed the crystal, it is time to take on the Ender Dragon. The best weapon to use is the bow. Wait until the Dragon is heading for you, and shoot for its head. Shooting the Dragon's head causes full damage. If you shoot it anywhere else, you will only give the Dragon about a quarter of the damage from your bow. You will need to do this over and over again, healing yourself as you get damaged. The Ender Dragon is immune to lava, potions, and fire. You can only damage the Ender Dragon with explosions or your sword or bow.

When you damage the Dragon, it flies off for a short while, and you can use this time to regroup and heal.

When you finally kill the Dragon, it explodes with impressive flashing rays. Its death creates an End exit portal for you to travel back to the Overworld, as well as a Dragon egg. The Dragon egg doesn't do anything itself. If you click it, it will teleport several blocks away, so it is very difficult to gather. (Hint: If you can get it to drop on a torch, it will turn into a collectible item.)

A dying Ender Dragon.

The End is a dark land, like the Nether, populated only by Endermen and the Ender Dragon. To get there, you must first find a portal, which is in a stronghold. Strongholds are complex mazes of dungeon-like rooms, corridors, and stairways, and there are only three in the Overworld. You'll find prison cells, libraries, and fountain rooms in a stronghold. To find a stronghold, you first gather fifteen or so Ender Pearls by killing Endermen. You craft these into Eyes of Ender using Blaze powder. (You can also trade with villagers for Eyes of Ender.) When you throw an Eye of Ender into the air, it will move in the direction of the nearest stronghold and then drop back to the ground. Pick up the Eye and travel in the direction it pointed. Every so often, throw another Eye into the sky to check your direction. When you are directly over the stronghold, the Eye you throw will fall and sink down into the ground. Now you dig! Once you reach the brick walls of the stronghold, you must break through and find the portal room, which has a silverfish spawner and a broken portal in it. The portal has places for Eyes of Ender to go in 12 frames along its border, but many are missing. You place your Eyes of Ender in the frames to fix the portal. Then you can jump in to travel to the End. Be prepared—the first time you visit the End you can return to the Overworld only by dying or killing the Dragon.

CHAPTER 15

ENDERMAN

Endermen are 3-block-tall black mobs with very long arms and legs. They wander about the Overworld and the End in their own little clouds of purple stars and occasionally pick up a block and hold it. (They're the reason your Minecraft neighborhood has all those little one-block holes in the ground!) They are neutral unless you provoke them, which happens by merely looking at them anywhere from their upper legs to their head. Moving the crosshair over these parts is considered looking, so it's not terribly difficult to avoid them, at least in the Overworld. You can look at their legs without a problem. There are so many Endermen in the End that avoiding looking at them is much more difficult.

ENDERMAN STATS

Mob Type: Neutral, Darkness

Health: 40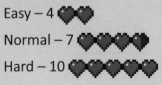

Attack Strength:

Easy – 4

Normal – 7

Hard – 10

Experience: 5

Drops: 0–1 Ender Pearls, used to make Eyes of Ender

Spawn: In light levels of 7 and less in the Overworld and in the End world

Sword Strikes to Kill:

Wood: 8

Stone: 7

Iron: 6

Gold: 8

Diamond: 5

Bow Strikes to Kill: 5

Fighting the Enderman

When you provoke an Enderman by looking at it or by attacking it, it will shudder and shake and make a very unsettling and long groan, like a disturbed airplane. It will teleport toward you suddenly and damage you by contact. When you attack it and it receives damage, it will teleport away and then back to you again, often behind you.

You can't use a bow, other projectiles, or a splash Potion of Harming on an Enderman, as it will teleport away before contact is made.

However, the Enderman has several weaknesses that you can use to your advantage.

- It can't pass under gaps less than three blocks high.

- Usually it doesn't teleport if you attack its lower legs.

- Contact with water causes damage.

- It becomes neutralized by damage from rain, lava, or sunlight.

If you are on the hunt for Ender Pearls and need to kill Endermen, make a little outpost with a 2-block high, 2-block deep gap you can fit into. Stare at an Enderman and nip into your outpost, keeping your back at the wall. When it teleports to you, attack only its legs with your sword. You'll get very little damage, if any, and quite possibly an Ender Pearl out of the deal.

You can defeat Endermen pretty easily by staying in a 2-block high gap and striking their feet.

You can also pillar 3 blocks up, stare at an Enderman, and strike it with your sword when it teleports close by. It can't teleport to your block or fly, so you can swing at it at your leisure. However, it's harder to swing just at its legs, so it may teleport away, leaving you Ender Pearl free.

CHAPTER 16

ENDERMITE

The Endermite is a new mob that came in the Minecraft 1.8 Bountiful Update. Its body is based a little on the silverfish. They look like tail-less, chubby, purple silverfish and, like the silverfish, they are low in health and attack damage. They can also jump up a block like silverfish, suffocate on soul sand, and make similar death squeals. As of 1.8, they only spawn rarely, when you use an Ender Pearl or when an Enderman teleports away. There may be changes to the Endermite in future updates, so keep an eye out!

ENDERMITE STATS

Mob Type: Hostile

Health: 8 ♥♥♥♥

Attack Strength: 2 ♥

Experience: 3

Drops: None

Spawn: There is a 5 percent chance that an Endermite will spawn when you throw an Ender Pearl. They can also spawn when an Enderman teleports away.

Sword Strikes to Kill:

Wood: 2

Stone: 2

Iron: 2

Gold: 2

Diamond: 1

Bow Strikes to Kill: 1

Fighting the Endermite

You can fight the Endermite with your sword at close quarters without having too much harm done to you. A few sword strikes will do it in, and it won't call any pals to help it out. However, they despawn after only a few minutes.

CHAPTER 17

GHAST

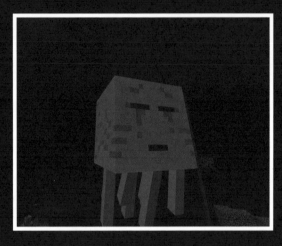

The Ghast is one of the largest mobs in Minecraft, with a body that is 4x4 blocks tall and 9 long, hanging tentacles. They float in the sky of the Nether, and if they see you and you are close enough, they will open their mouths to emit a fireball aimed right at you. You can tell if a Ghast is around by the mewling, catlike cry it makes. Like other Nether creatures, they are not damaged by fire or lava.

GHAST STATS

Mob Type:	Hostile, Nether
Health:	10 ❤❤❤❤❤
Attack Strength:	Max 17 ❤❤❤❤❤❤❤❤❤
	Damage depends on how far away

the Ghast is and where the player
is in the explosion radius.

Experience: 5

Drops: 0–2 gunpowder, 0–1 Ghast tears

Spawn: In the Nether.

Sword Strikes to Kill:

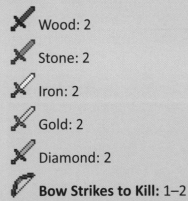 Wood: 2

Stone: 2

Iron: 2

Gold: 2

Diamond: 2

Bow Strikes to Kill: 1–2

Fighting the Ghast

The Ghast can shoot from a very long range—up to 100 blocks—
but it won't shoot its fireballs at you unless it has line of sight
to you. The fireballs aren't very fast, so you have some time to
hide, if that's what you want to do.

Otherwise, fire up your bow, as that is the easiest way to kill a
Ghast. They don't usually come too close. To protect yourself,
you can build a cobblestone or obsidian wall to nip behind. As
the Ghast fires at you, the fireballs will catch Netherrack near
you on fire, and this is almost as dangerous. If you can create a

cobblestone area to fight from, this can help. If the Ghast is far away, make sure to aim high.

You can also bounce its fireball right back at the Ghast. The fireball travels slowly, so you have enough time to punch it back with your bow or your sword. You can even use your fist and not be damaged or shoot an arrow at the fireball. If you aim the punch just right, you can send the fireball right back to the Ghast, killing it *and* getting the achievement Return to Sender.

A Ghast opens its eyes and mouth right before firing.

It is difficult to get the Ghast drop, a Ghast tear. This is used to make the very handy Potion of Regeneration. Typically, the Ghast will be flying over lava when your arrow hits it, and its drops will land in the lava and burn up. One solution is to hook the Ghast with your fishing rod, draw it toward you, and then attack it with your sword once it is over land. Use a sword enchanted with Looting to maximize your plunder.

CHAPTER 18

GUARDIAN

The Guardian is a brand new mob introduced with the Minecraft 1.8 Bountiful Update. It and the Elder Guardian are the only two hostile mobs of the sea. Guardians spawn nearby a new structure called the ocean monument. An ocean monument is similar to the desert temple and jungle temple, although there are no chests inside. There is a central treasure room in the ocean monument, where 8 gold blocks are hidden behind dark prismarine blocks.

GUARDIAN STATS

Mob Type: Hostile, Local

Health: 30 ♥♥♥♥♥♥♥♥♥♥♥♥♥♥♥

Attack Strength:

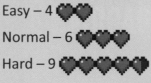

Easy – 4

Normal – 6

Hard – 9

Experience: 10

Drops: 1–2 raw fish, 0–2 prismarine shards, 0–1 prismarine crystals.

Spawn: In the ocean by ocean monuments.

Sword Strikes to Kill:

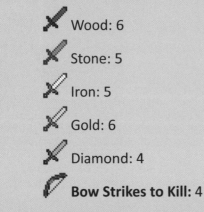

Wood: 6

Stone: 5

Iron: 5

Gold: 6

Diamond: 4

Bow Strikes to Kill: 4

Fighting the Guardian

Because you'll be fighting underwater, you will need to prepare armor and potions that will help you breathe, see, and move quickly beneath the ocean surface.

The Guardian swims suddenly and quickly in and around its ocean monument, attacking players and squid. It attacks by firing its laser at you. However, first it must charge its laser; while this is happening, the laser is purple and does no damage. Then, when it is fully charged, the beam turns yellow, delivers its blow, and stops. A few seconds pass before the Guardian can recharge. The laser can reach about 15 blocks to hit you, as long as there are no solid blocks between the Guardian and you. In addition, if you attack the Guardian while its spikes are out, it will deal you 2 points of damage.

Guardians zap you with rays to damage you.

Wearing armor and enchanted armor can help protect you from the Guardian's laser. It might seem best to stay at a distance and use your bow and arrow. However, arrows don't travel well underwater, and the Guardian moves quickly. It can easily dart out of the way and zap you. Your best tactic is to be aggressive and fast. Corner the Guardian so that it can't escape you, and attack it quickly with the sharpest sword you have.

CHAPTER 19

KILLER BUNNY

The Killer Bunny is a type of rabbit, a new mob introduced with the Minecraft 1.8 Bountiful Update. Rabbits themselves are passive mobs, of course. As you might expect, they are skilled at hopping and eating carrots. The Killer Bunny is spawned very rarely and randomly. It is a white rabbit the same size as others. However, it has horizontal red eyes and displays the name "The Killer Bunny." You can find normal white rabbits with vertical red eyes, but these aren't hostile. The Killer Bunny is hostile to players and all wolves, but will attack players first before wolves. If it spots you within a 15-block radius, it will leap straight toward you.

KILLER BUNNY STATS

Mob Type: Hostile

Health: 10 ♥♥♥♥♥

Attack Strength:

Easy – 5
Normal – 8
Hard – 12

Experience: 1–3

Drops: 0–1 raw rabbit, 0–1 rabbit hide, (less commonly) rabbit's foot

Spawn: Killer Bunnies have a one in a thousand chance of spawning instead of a normal rabbit. Like rabbits, they'll spawn in the savannah, plains, swamp, extreme hills, birch forest, and other forested biomes.

Sword Strikes to Kill:

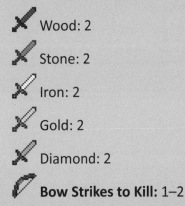

Wood: 2

Stone: 2

Iron: 2

Gold: 2

Diamond: 2

Bow Strikes to Kill: 1–2

Fighting the Killer Bunny

If the Killer Bunny takes you by surprise, it can really knock you back and deal you a hard blow. However, it is pretty easy to kill: just two swipes of any sword should do it.

CHAPTER 20

MAGMA CUBE

Magma cubes are a square 2x2 mob that bounce. They have dark red and black skin and yellow and red eyes. Their accordion-like body expands as they hop up and retracts when they hit the ground.

MAGMA CUBE STATS

Mob Type: Hostile, Nether

Health*:

          Large – 16 pts ♥♥♥♥♥♥♥♥

          Medium – 4 ♥♥

          Tiny – 1 ♥

*Magma cubes also have hidden armor points, which protect them against up to nearly 50 percent of the damage you cause. This means their health, in practice, is higher than the number of hearts they have, and it will take more strikes to kill them.

Attack Strength:

Large – 6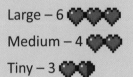

Medium – 4

Tiny – 3

Drops: 0–1 magma cream (only medium and large magma cubes drop these)

Spawn: In the Nether.

Sword Strikes to Kill (Large):

 Wood: 4

Stone: 3

Iron: 3

Gold: 4

Diamond: 2

Bow Strikes to Kill: 2

Fighting the Magma Cube

The most difficult thing about fighting mobs in the Nether is your location. There are cliffs of Netherrack with dangerous and life-threatening drops, and lava seas, pools, and dripping columns are everywhere. Half the battle is making sure you are somewhere relatively safe and aren't backing up to a drop into lava. You can increase your chances by using Fire Protection enchantments on your armor and Feather Falling on your boots.

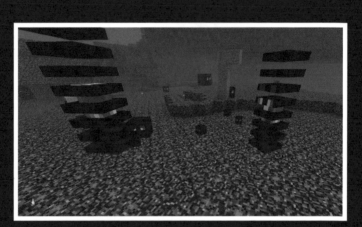

Magma cubes jumping.

Magma cubes are similar to their Overworld cousins, slimes. If you kill a large cube, it spawns 4 medium-sized ones. And when you kill a medium-sized cube, it spawns four tiny cubes. If you are using a diamond sword on a large magma cube, it won't take long to kill. However, if you don't have a diamond sword, an iron sword with Knockback enchantment is a very good alternative. The cube keeps bouncing toward you, and it damages you if it lands on top of you. Knockback helps propel the cube backward so it can't land on you. If it is jumping over you, you still have a chance to stab it with your sword while it is over you. Magma cubes are slow enough that you can take them out with a bow and arrow. The smaller cubes move slowly and have low enough health that it isn't too hard to exterminate them pretty quickly.

SILVERFISH

T he silverfish lives in strongholds and in stone blocks in the extreme hills biome. It's one of Minecraft's smallest mobs, taking up less space than a block. However, a silverfish can jump 1 block high and can push a player. It will scurry with a wiggling motion straight to you and inflict 1 point of damage when it touches or pushes you. That's not so bad, compared to other hostile mobs. However, if you attack a silverfish directly, with a weapon, other silverfish nearby (within about 10 blocks) may be woken up and come to join the first silverfish in attacking you back. A silverfish can also disappear into another stone block, making it into a monster egg.

Silverfish will suffocate if they are on a patch of soul sand that is too big (around 5x5 blocks or larger) for them to hustle off. If they are on just one block of soul sand, they can usually get off the block before they die.

SILVERFISH STATS

Mob Type: Hostile, Local

Health: 8

Attack Strength: 1

Experience: 5

Drops: None

Spawn: From silverfish spawners in strongholds and in monster eggs (also called silverfish stone) in extreme hills biomes. With a spawner, silverfish can spawn on stone blocks at any light level, but on non-stone blocks only at light level 11 or lower. They can't spawn within 5 blocks of a player.

Sword Strikes to Kill:

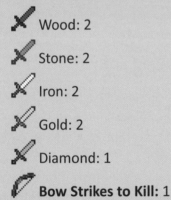

Wood: 2

Stone: 2

Iron: 2

Gold: 2

Diamond: 1

Bow Strikes to Kill: 1

Fighting the Silverfish

In general, the silverfish's low health and mild attack strength make it easy to kill quickly. If you kill a silverfish in one hit, which you can do with a diamond sword, it won't awaken the other silverfish hiding in monster eggs nearby. You can also enchant a diamond or iron pickaxe with Sharpness, so that it gives 8 or more attack damage, and use that for mining in extreme hills. That way, when a silverfish emerges, you can give it one swing with your pickaxe and continue mining.

One silverfish is easy to kill, but a swarm can overtake you.

If you don't have a diamond sword or enchanted pickaxe, use an indirect way to kill the silverfish, so that it doesn't wake up other silverfish. Jump on a short pillar of gravel (2 high), and drop lava or gravel on it. To suffocate the silverfish with gravel, you do have to place the gravel against a wall or pillar block so that it can slide down directly on top the silverfish. The silverfish gives a nice, long death squeal when you do this! However, because you need to place the gravel carefully so that it suffocates the silverfish, the better solution is a bucket of lava. You can also use flint and steel very handily to set a single silverfish ablaze. It will die without awakening others.

Although one silverfish by itself is not very harmful, a swarm of silverfish can quickly kill you. If you awaken a swarm of silverfish, you will definitely want to pillar up so that they cannot get to you. When you are mining in extreme hills, make sure you have a short stack of gravel on hand and a bucket of lava.

Whatever you do, don't attack the silverfish with a splash potion, especially a splash Potion of Poison. A Potion of Poison makes multiple "attacks," and with each attack, more silverfish are alerted and you could end up with a very large swarm. A Potion of Harming gives an instant effect so you can kill one silverfish with one splash. However, if there are several silverfish present, some may not be killed by the splash and are then able to summon others.

Mining Monster Eggs

Monster eggs can look like any of the stone blocks: cobblestone, stone, stone brick, cracked stone bricks, mossy stone bricks, or chiseled stone. In an extreme hills biome, they'll appear as stone. However, monster eggs take noticeably longer to mine with a pickaxe than a regular stone block. Once you've mined a few, you'll be able to tell while you are striking a stone block if it is a monster egg. (If you use your hands, monster eggs are actually faster to mine than stone.) When you've woken a silverfish from its egg, a little white cloud appears that looks like the cloud that forms when you kill a mob.

CHAPTER 22

SKELETON

The skelly is one of the big four—the four common mobs of the Minecraft Overworld (the others are the zombie, the spider, and the Creeper) that you'll see daily. When a skeleton is near, you will hear the tinkly sound of bones rattling together.

Although skeletons spawn with a bow, some are able to pick up weapons. If they pick up a more damaging sword, they'll use that instead. Some skeletons spawn with armor or enchanted bows, which will make them harder to kill.

If they are within 16 blocks of you, they will chase you; when they are within 8 blocks of you, they'll start shooting their bows. If you get 16 blocks away from them again, they'll lose interest in you.

As of the Minecraft 1.8 Bountiful Update, skeletons are afraid of wolves (as they should be!). All wolves now chase and attack skeletons without provocation, and the skeleton will run away when it sees a wolf. They will also now run away from a Creeper that is gearing up to explode.

SKELETON STATS

Mob Type: Hostile, Darkness

Health: 20 ♥♥♥♥♥♥♥♥♥♥

Attack Strength (Bow):

Easy – 1 ♥

Normal – 2 ♥

Hard – 4 ♥♥

Attack Strength (Sword):

Easy – 2 ♥

Normal – 2 ♥

Hard – 3 ♥♥

Experience: 5

Drops: 0–2 arrows, more rarely bows and armor (which may be enchanted, but usually badly damaged), 1 skeleton skull (if killed by a charged Creeper)

Spawn: In Overworld at light levels 7 and below, and by skeleton spawners found in dungeons. Also spawns more rarely in the Nether, near Nether fortresses.

Sword Strikes to Kill:

Wood: 4

Stone: 4

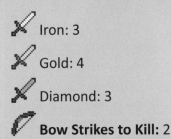

Iron: 3

Gold: 4

Diamond: 3

Bow Strikes to Kill: 2

Fighting the Skeleton

When a skeleton attacks you, it fires its arrows more rapidly the closer it gets. With the knockback of an arrow hit from it, you'll find it is difficult to get close enough to use a sword, and you can be hit multiple times while you're trying to do so. To avoid being hit by the skeleton, strafe. Use your left and right move keys (A and D) to move left and right. The one thing you don't want to do with a skeleton is knock it back by sprinting and striking it with your sword. This knock back actually gives the skeleton more time to charge and fire its bow.

If you are mining in a cave and you've captured a skeleton's attention, draw it to a location where there are some blocks you can hide behind. When it starts coming around the corner of the block, attack the edge of it before it fully emerges. As with other mob attacks, use the blocking technique to limit the damage the skeleton does.

Skeletons and other mobs are more likely to spawn with armor, weapons, and enchantments in Hard difficulty or when it is a full moon.

Skeletons burn in the daylight, unless they are wearing a helmet or a pumpkin (or are in water), so one passive tactic is to try to draw them out into the open during the day. Once they've taken some damage, finish them off with your sword or bow so you can reap the rewards of dropped loot.

Skeletons are not solid, which leads to an interesting scenario. If you are close to one, and its back is against a wall, walk right up into the block it is standing in. You are now inside the skeleton and can hit it with your sword. Meanwhile, all the skelly can do is fire its arrows meaninglessly into the ground. Score!

CHAPTER 23

SLIME

The slime is a large (2x2x2 blocks) cubed mob. It's green, very slightly transparent, and makes a squelchy sound as it hops straight toward you. When you kill the large slime, it breaks into up to four smaller ones. These split into up to four tiny ones when you kill them.

There are two good things about slimes. One, they're not too fast and not too strong, so they're not difficult to kill. Second, they provide slimeballs as a drop, which you can use to make magma cream, leads to tie animals to posts, sticky pistons, and slime blocks you can bounce on.

Slimes are actually relatively rare. In swamps, they will only spawn at night where the light is 7 or below. The moon also affects when they spawn. They spawn more during a full moon and not at all during a new moon. They can also spawn at any light levels at lower depths of the world (levels 0–39), but only under special conditions and in 1 of about 10 chunks. A chunk is a segment of the Minecraft world that is 16 blocks square and the full height of the world, 256 blocks. Chunks are used in the programming code to manage mobs spawning and despawning and rendering, among other things.

SLIME STATS

Mob Type: Hostile, Local

Health:

> Big – 16
>
> Small – 4
>
> Tiny – 1

Attack Strength:

> Big – 4 pts
>
> Small – 2 pts
>
> Tiny – 0

Experience:

> Big – 4
>
> Small – 2
>
> Tiny – 1

Drops: 0–2 slimeballs, from tiny slime

Spawn: Swamps in low light and in levels below 40.

Sword Strikes to Kill (Big Slime):

> Wood: 4
>
> Stone: 3

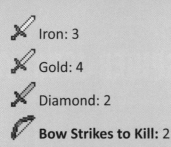

⚔ Iron: 3

⚔ Gold: 4

⚔ Diamond: 2

🏹 **Bow Strikes to Kill:** 2

Fighting the Slime

Slimes are not very difficult to kill. Use your sword and click fast. Although the smaller slimes will seem like they can overtake you, they are very easy to kill. You can punch a tiny slime with your fist and it will die and give you a slimeball for your effort. Overall, they are mostly just a hindrance, especially if you are mining and come across a slime-generating chunk. When you do, block off your mining corridors to leave just one-block gaps that only the smaller slimes can get through.

Killing a large or medium slime will spawn up to four additional smaller slimes.

CHAPTER 24

SPIDERS AND SPIDER JOCKEYS

ou can always tell when a spider is nearby because of its typical scratchy hiss. (If you can hear one but can't see it, it's probably just overhead, in a tree or on your roof.) Spiders are neutral at higher, daylight levels of light. In the dark, at light levels of 7 and below, they become hostile. And once hostile, they never revert back to neutral.

Spiders are very agile, and they can move quickly and jump across a 3- or 4-block gap. They can also climb up vertical blocks, as if the blocks had ladders attached. Spiders are two blocks wide, so they can't fit through 1x1 gaps. They do fit through 1 high x 2 wide spaces, though.

Before the latest 1.8 Bountiful Update, spiders could see and track you through walls. With 1.8, they can no longer do this.

If you are playing on Hard mode, spiders can sometimes spawn with a status effect. A status effect is a special ability, usually delivered through a potion. Spiders in Hard mode can spawn with Invisibility, Regeneration, Strength, or Swiftness effects that are pretty much permanent.

SPIDER STATS

Type: Neutral (Hostile at low light levels)

Health: 16

Attack strength:

> Easy – 2 🖤
>
> Normal – 2 🖤
>
> Hard – 3 🖤🖤

Experience: 5

Drops: 0–2 string, 0–1 spider eye

Spawn: In the Overworld, in light levels of 7 or less, and in dungeons from spider spawners.

Sword Strikes to Kill:

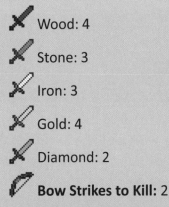

🗡 Wood: 4

🗡 Stone: 3

🗡 Iron: 3

🗡 Gold: 4

🗡 Diamond: 2

🏹 **Bow Strikes to Kill:** 2

Fighting the Spider

Because spiders are fast, the best way to kill them is with a bow and arrow, if you have the chance. If you must use a sword, first try to make sure you are on higher ground than the spider. If the spider is above you, it can jump on top of you and cause extra damage. If you can't get to higher ground, move to a flatter area so that the spider at least isn't above you.

You can also use flint and steel to set a spider alight. Make sure you are a couple blocks away so you don't catch on fire also! For extra power against the spider, enchant your sword with the Bane of Arthropods enchantment, as this will deliver extra damage to spiders. If you are doing well with experience levels and can enchant extra swords, you can enchant one sword to use while mining.

You can also use the width of the spider to your advantage to slip through a 1-block wide gap and attack the spider through the gap. Overall, the spider has lower health than the other four common mobs (zombie, skeleton, and Creeper, which all have 20 points of health), so it is a bit easier to defeat.

Beware the Spider Jockey

Very rarely, a spider will spawn with a skeleton riding on its shoulders. About 1 in 100 spiders spawn this way. This hybrid monster is called a spider jockey and is a deadly combination. It carries all the attack strength of both a spider and skeleton put together. It has the climbing ability of a spider and the accurate aim of the skeleton. However, you will have to kill each one of them separately, and each will provide its separate drops: arrows and bones or string and spider eyes.

Ideally, when you spot a spider jockey, you will run away and hide, so as to preserve your life. If you have enchanted weaponry and armor though, or are confident in your combat skills, you can be bolder. Use your bow and arrow, first to kill the skeleton on top and then the spider.

About 1 in 100 spiders spawn with a skeleton rider.

CHAPTER 25

WITCH

itches look a lot like villagers, except for their tall black hats, purple cloaks, and grayish skin. Their noses are big like a villager's, but a witch's nose can wiggle and has one large wart on it. Despite their good looks and charm, witches are one of the most harmful mobs you encounter in the Overworld on a normal day. If you are low on health, it might be best to avoid them, as they are difficult to kill and can inflict a lot of damage. They are difficult to kill because they heal themselves while you are fighting them. They use helpful potions on themselves and throw harmful potions at you.

When witches were first introduced in the game, they only spawned in witch huts. Witch huts are small wooden homes raised above the water in swamps. A witch still spawns with a witch hut, but they can also spawn anywhere in the Overworld where there is a light level 7 or below, so you may find one in your spelunking expeditions. And if a villager is struck by lightning, it turns into a witch.

WITCH STATS

Mob Type: Hostile, Local

Health: 26

Attack Strength: Witches attack you through potions, and two will cause damage to your health (the Potion of Poison and Potion of Harming). One potion of poison can cause up 38 or more points of damage but will always leave you with 1 point of health, so it won't kill you. A Potion of Harming can cause up to 12 points of health.

Experience: 5

Drops: 0–6 sticks, 0–6 gunpowder, 0–6 sugar, 0–6 spider eyes, 0–6 glowstone dust, 0–6 redstone, 0–6 glass bottles, (more rarely) 1 potion (Healing, Fire Resistance, Swiftness, or Water Breathing)

Spawn: In the Overworld at light levels 7 or less and witch huts in the Swamp biome. With the 1.8 Minecraft Bountiful Update, villagers who are struck by lightning will turn into witches.

Sword Strikes to Kill:

 Wood: 6

Stone: 5

Iron: 4

Gold: 6

Diamond: 4

Bow Strikes to Kill: 3

Fighting the Witch

There is a logic to what potions witches will throw at you and when. When you are within 8 blocks of a witch, it will throw a Potion of Slowness at you to slow you down, unless you already are under a Slowness status effect. If you don't retreat, and your health is 8 points or over, they'll throw a Potion of Poison at you. Poison won't kill you, but it can take you down to a single point of health (half a heart). Then, if you get within 3 blocks of a witch, they sometimes throw a Potion of Weakness, as long as you aren't already inflicted with a Weakness effect. Finally, once you have been inflicted by Slowness and Poison, they'll start throwing Potions of Harming. These can and will kill you.

Meanwhile, as soon as the witch sees you, the witch drinks potions to heal itself. They'll guzzle a Potion of Healing when they're damaged and a Potion of Fire Resistance if they're on fire. If they're underwater, they can drink a Potion of Water Breathing. Also, if they are 12 or so blocks away from you, they can drink a Potion of Swiftness so they can quickly get close to you before they attack.

This witch has just drunk a Potion of Healing and thrown a Potion of Slowness.

The best way to fight a witch is to use your bow and arrow from a distance. The bow has a longer range than a witch throwing splash potions, so you can come out of the battle completely unscathed. If long range is not an option, your best bet is to rush the witch immediately. If you can, surprise them by keeping hidden as long as possible. Get in as many strikes with your sword as you can before they start drinking their Potion of Healing. (You can tell they're drinking their potion by the bubbles floating up from them.) You can kill a witch quickly with fast swordplay before they even get around to throwing the Potion of Harming.

When you do kill them, they'll drop materials from potion making, sometimes a stick (perhaps from their unseen broomstick?) and, more rarely, a potion that they were about to drink.

CHAPTER 26

THE WITHER

The Wither is an extremely powerful boss mob. It is the only hostile mob in the Minecraft game that the player creates. To create a Wither, you must have been to the Nether to collect soul sand and three wither skeleton skulls. You arrange the soul sand blocks in a T-shape and then place the skulls on the top three blocks. When the last skull is placed, the blocks turn into the Wither boss mob. You must place one skull as the last block or the Wither won't spawn.

The spawning of the Wither is a dramatic event. The sky turns slightly darker, and the Wither flashes blue. It grows larger and larger, gaining health. (Like the other boss mob, the Ender Dragon, the Wither's health bar will show on your screen.) During this period, it is immune to any attacks. Finally, when its full health is reached, the Wither flashes and creates a giant explosion around itself and changes into its final, somewhat larger form. A black, flying, skeleton-like, three-headed, projectile-hurling hostile form. The Wither immediately and constantly attacks any living entities it sees—you, a cow, everything—flying from target to target. The projectiles it hurls are Wither skulls. There are two types of Wither skull it can throw: fast black ones and slower, rarer blue skulls. Both have the same explosive power as Ghast fireballs. The black skulls can't explode hard blocks like cobblestone, while the blue skulls can break all blocks except for bedrock and the End portal frame. So the Wither causes a lot of destruction—to the world around you and to you.

THE WITHER STATS

Mob Type: Boss

Health: 300  x 15

Armor Points: 4 🛡️🛡️

Attack Strength:

Easy – 5 ❤️❤️🖤

Normal – 8 ❤️❤️❤️❤️

Hard – 12 ❤️❤️❤️❤️❤️❤️

(On Normal and Hard, the Wither attack also gives Wither effect, which is similar to poison.)

Experience: 50

Drops: 1 Nether star

Spawn: Initiated by player.

Sword Strikes to Kill:

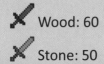 Wood: 60

Stone: 50

Iron: 43

Gold: 60

Diamond: 38

Bow Strikes to Kill: 34

Fighting the Wither

There are quite a few reasons not to create and fight the Wither. (1) The Wither has 100 more points of health than the Ender Dragon. (2) It can throw three Wither skulls at a time, some of which can destroy any blocks except bedrock. (3) Besides blast damage, Wither skulls also inflict the Wither effect on you. This drains your health and also makes it difficult to see what your health is because it turns your health bar black. (4) Inflicting the Wither effect on you actually heals the Wither by 5 points. (5) It is immune to fire and lava. (6) If you get the Wither down to half health, it suddenly gets Wither armor protection, which makes it immune to arrows. (It can't fly at this point, which is a plus.) (7) The only potion you can use against a Wither is the Potion of Healing, as it is an undead mob.

There are two reasons to fight the Wither yourself: (1) for the bragging rights and (2) for the ultra rare drop, a single Nether star. Killing the Wither is the only way to get a Nether star, and a Nether star is the key ingredient for creating beacons. Beacons are made of glass, Nether star, and obsidian. In addition to making a powerful light beam, if you place a beacon on a pyramid of iron, diamond, emerald, or gold, you can give yourself and anyone nearby the beacon special status effect powers.

To take on the Wither, you must have enchanted armor and weapons. You won't survive without it, and you'll pretty likely die even with it. You can make it much easier on yourself if you go to the End and defeat the Ender Dragon first. Then you can go back to the End to stage your Wither battle there. In the End, the Wither will also attack Endermen, who will join in the fight. They will help you get the Wither to half health, when at least it can't fly any more.

Regardless, you will want to stage your battle away from your home base, to protect it from the massive explosive destruction that will be caused. Enlist any help you can, from other players on multiplayer servers or by building iron golems. Use obsidian to create a safe area, and to protect the extra armor, weapons, and potions you will need. If possible, create a special space, walled with obsidian, to confine your battle and reduce unnecessary amounts of flying about and chasing.

The Wither firing an explosive skull at you.

Your bow should be enchanted with the highest Power and Punch level you can afford, as well as Infinity. Your sword, also, should be enchanted with the highest Smite level, along with Knockback. (Looting won't help deliver more Nether stars.) In addition, brew multiple bottles of Potion of Healing, both for yourself and to harm the Wither, along with several Golden Apples, and some Potions of Strength, Regeneration, and Swiftness. For your armor, get the highest level of Blast Protection, if you can. Before your battle, eat an enchanted apple and drink your Strength, Swiftness, and Regen potions. Use your bow for the first half of the battle, then when the Wither is no longer flying, use your sword. Good luck!

CHAPTER 27

WITHER SKELETON

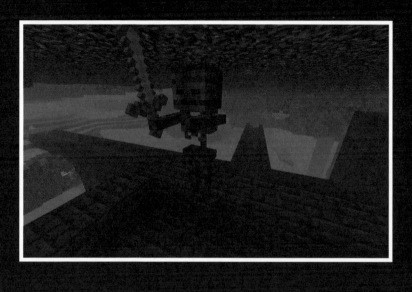

Wither skeletons look similar to regular Overworld skeletons, but they are 2.5 blocks high instead of 2. Their bones are a dark grayish black. They only spawn in the Nether, in or by Nether fortresses. The mouth of a Wither skeleton is not as wide as a regular skeleton. Whereas skeletons are equipped with a bow, the Wither skeleton carries a stone sword. Like skeletons, Wither skeletons will run away from wolves and can pick up armor and weapons. Unlike Overworld skeletons, they won't burn in daylight. They will flash with fire for a moment, but they aren't killed or damaged. They aren't damaged at all by either lava or fire, because they are natives of the Hell biome of the Nether.

Wither skeletons strike you with their sword, which gives you the Wither effect, similar to poisoning. The Wither effect lasts

10 seconds and gives 1 point of damage every couple of seconds. When you've received the Wither effect, your health bar turns black. You can heal yourself with milk, potions, and the like. Wither skeleton attacks will knock you back, so be especially careful if you are near cliffs or ledges. Also beware if one picks up a bow, as it will use the bow, and the arrows will be on fire.

WITHER SKELETON STATS

Mob Type: Hostile, Nether, Local

Health: 20

Attack Strength:

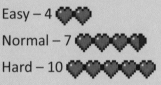

Easy – 4

Normal – 7

Hard – 10

Experience: 5

Drops: 0–1 coal, 0–2 bones, (more rarely) a stone sword or 1 Wither skeleton skull, used to create a Wither boss. A Wither skeleton is more likely to drop a skull if it's killed by a charged creeper.

Spawn: In or near Nether fortresses at light level 7 or lower.

Sword Strikes to Kill:

Wood: 4

Stone: 4

Iron: 3

Gold: 4

Diamond: 3

Fighting the Wither Skeleton

Wither skeletons move fast. They walk as fast as a player and also can sprint. And because they can deal a fairly large amount of damage to you, it is best to be prepared and plan safe places or escape routes, especially if you are visiting the Nether without powerfully enchanted weapons and armor. For example, because Wither skeletons can't pass through 2-high blocks, you can place blocks on fortress corridor ceilings to prevent them from following you. Have Potions of Healing or Regeneration at the ready.

First, at a distance (12 blocks or so), use a bow enchanted with Power as well as Punch. Punch will knock back the target, which can buy you some more time. Closer to the skeleton, use your sword. Once you are close, though, it is highly likely that this mob will give you the Wither effect. You'll want to keep a melee as short as possible, so use a diamond sword enchanted with Sharpness or Smite. The Smite enchantment is even more damaging to undead mobs than the Sharpness enchantment, so if you can spare an extra sword to use just against the undead, do so. (However, you'll often find Blazes and Wither skeletons nearby or together, and the Smite enchantment doesn't work against blazes.)

That said, the most powerful enchantment for damaging your enemy is Smite V or Sharpness V. A diamond sword with either of these will kill a Wither skeleton in one strike. With Smite IV or with Sharpness IV, you'll need just two strokes to kill it. Because Wither skeleton skulls are rare and essential for creating a Wither, try to use a Looting enchanted sword to improve your chances of getting a skull.

If you can't kill the Wither skeleton in one stroke, retreat to or make a 2-high block that it can't enter. Draw it near you, attack with your sword, then quickly move back into your safe zone out of range of their sword. Heal if you need to, and repeat.

A Wither skeleton standing next to its cousin, the regular skeleton.

CHAPTER 28

WOLF

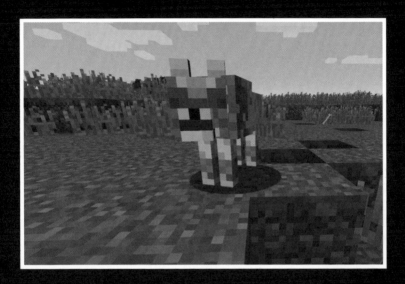

wolf can exist in three states: wild, tamed, and hostile. A wild wolf is grayish and its tail droops down. A hostile wolf has red eyes and makes snarling or growling sounds. A tamed wolf has lighter fur, its tail angles up, and it has a collar.

Wild wolves are neutral and won't attack you. They live in small groups, or packs, and attack sheep and rabbits. All wolves, including tame ones, will also attack skeletons without being attacked first by them. However, if you attack a wild wolf, all wild wolves nearby will turn hostile and attack you. They will continue to be hostile and attack you until you die. A tamed wolf never becomes hostile to players.

WOLF STATS

Mob Type: Neutral

Health:

Wild – 8 ♥♥♥♥

Tame – 20 ♥♥♥♥♥♥♥♥♥♥

Attack Strength (Wild):

Easy – 3 ♥♥

Normal – 4 ♥♥

Hard – 6 ♥♥♥

Attack Strength (Tamed): 4 ♥♥

Experience: 1–3

Drops: None

Spawn: In Forest and Taiga biomes.

Sword Strikes to Kill (Wild):

Wood: 2

Stone: 2

Iron: 2

Gold: 2

Diamond: 1

Bow Strikes to Kill (Wild): 1

A hostile wolf's tail sticks straight out and it has red eyes, an unprovoked wild wolf's tail points down, and a healthy tamed wolf's tail points up.

Fighting the Wolf

It's much smarter to never attack a wolf, because wolves remain hostile and they attack as a group. If, for some reason, you have inadvertently damaged a wolf and a pack is now after you, your best tactic is to escape. If you can, tunnel away and make sure to close off your tunnel's entrance! You'll need torches to light your way, of course. A hostile mob has a chance of despawning or disappearing from the game if it isn't within 32 blocks of a player for more than half a minute. They will definitely despawn if they are more than 128 blocks from a player. So tunnel away for at least 128 blocks before you come out.

CHAPTER 29

ZOMBIE

It's hard to make it through a night without seeing a zombie or a morning without seeing a zombie go up in flames. If you see one alight, strike it fast for a final death blow so you can get the XP.

Zombies are the most common hostile mob in Minecraft. In case you haven't noticed, the zombies look a bit like Steve with a turquoise T-shirt and blue pants. (There's a story in there somewhere!)

Some zombies spawn as zombie villagers, which have the same face as a villager, just green. And if a zombie attacks a villager, it will turn the villager into a zombie villager. There's also another type of zombie, the baby zombie, which you can read about in the baby zombie chapter.

ZOMBIE STATS

Mob type: Hostile, Darkness

Health: 20 ♥♥♥♥♥♥♥♥♥♥

Attack Strength:

Easy – 2 ♥

Normal – 4 ♥♥

Hard – 5 ♥♥♥

Experience: 5

Drops: 0–2 rotten flesh, (more rarely) a carrot, iron ingot, potato, armor and weapons (if they holding them), a zombie head (if they are killed by a charged creeper)

Spawn: In Overworld in light levels of 7 or lower.

Sword Strikes to Kill:

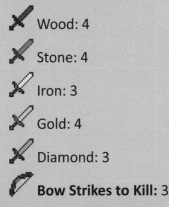

Wood: 4

Stone: 4

Iron: 3

Gold: 4

Diamond: 3

Bow Strikes to Kill: 3

Fighting the Zombie

If you don't want to fight a zombie, just draw it into sunlight (if its day and you're not in a cave!). However, of all the common mobs, zombies are probably the easiest to defeat. They let you know pretty clearly when they're nearby with some good loud groans, and they move pretty slowly. If there's water between you and the zombie, it will take forever to get to you! And as you know, they will burn and die in sunlight (unless they are in water), making them a darkness-only pest.

A villager zombie
burning up in the sun.

Zombies can spawn with armor, an iron shovel, or an iron sword. They can also pick up and wear armor, including mob heads dropped by a charged Creeper killing another zombie, skeleton, or Creeper. (This means you could find a zombie wearing a creeper head!) In any case, with armor, zombies become more difficult to kill, and while wearing a helmet they will not burn in the sun. Also, if you are playing on Hard mode, injuring one zombie will cause others to come help attack you.

A zombie with an enchanted shovel!

Use a bow and arrow to kill a zombie from a distance and you'll suffer no damage, as they can only attack you at close range. Face to face, you should be able to knock a zombie out with your sword pretty easily; a sword enchanted with Knockback can also help.

CHAPTER 30

ZOMBIE PIGMAN

The zombie pigman is a very common mob in the Nether, but they are neutral. This means that if you ignore them, they will ignore you. And that is usually the best course of action. You can occasionally find them in the Overworld, as they can spawn near Nether portals. In the very rare chance that an Overworld pig is struck by lightning, it will turn into a zombie pigman, though without a sword.

ZOMBIE PIGMAN STATS

Mob Type: Neutral, Nether

Health: 20 ♥♥♥♥♥♥♥♥♥♥

Attack Strength:

Easy – 5

Normal – 9

Hard – 13

Experience: 5

Drops: 0–2 Rotten flesh, 0–1 gold nuggets, (more rarely) gold swords and gold ingots

Spawn: In the Nether at any light level and in the Overworld by a Nether portal or when lightning strikes close to a pig.

Sword Strikes to Kill*:

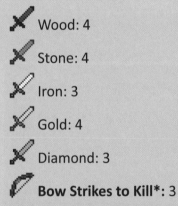

Wood: 4

Stone: 4

Iron: 3

Gold: 4

Diamond: 3

Bow Strikes to Kill*: 3

*The zombie pigman also has 2 armor points, which means you will need more strikes to kill it.

Fighting the Zombie Pigman

As with all neutral mobs, it's better to avoid fighting with zombie pigmen. Any zombie pigman within 32 blocks of you (after you've attacked one of their kind) will be provoked, and if you get within 16 blocks they will chase and attack you. The only way to escape is to sprint (if you have a clear escape route), use a Potion of Swiftness, or ride away on a horse. If you must, try to use a bow from far away, so swarms won't attack you. If you've inadvertently struck one, and there are others about, try to dig into Netherrack and down a little bit. Close the gap behind you, but leave a 1-block high gap at the pigman's foot level. This should allow you to hack away at their feet, killing them. When the mob stops coming for you, or when you get tired of killing them, tunnel 128 blocks away in one direction to despawn them. When you return, new pigmen who know nothing about the fight will spawn and leave you alone.

If you attack one zombie pigman, all the pigmen nearby will come in a horde to attack you.